©The Life Graduate Publishing Group 2020

No part of this book may be scanned, reproduced or distributed in any printed or electronic form without the prior permission of the author or publisher.

www.thelifegraduate.com

Information for Parents

The development of fine motor skills, like writing, aids in improving reading speed and accuracy for young children.

As your child progresses from using larger items like crayons, large pencils, or marker pens, the development of writing becomes an important developmental skill for all children.

This book will help your child to:
- Gain exposure to letters from the alphabet.
- Become aware of the shapes and structures of each letter and number.
- Develop writing muscle memory with the development of fine motor skill developed through repetition.
- Assist children in getting to know the alphabet and learn basic word structures.

This book has been designed in progressive stages so the child can build confidence throughout each section. The child will initially focus on straight lines and shapes with tracing patterns and interactive activities then progress to letters and shapes beginning with capital letters and then lower case letters.

We are excited to help your child on their educational journey as they learn to write, and we hope your child has fun along the journey by using this book.

 # CONTENTS

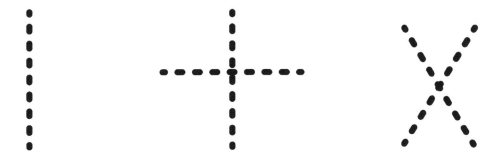

SECTION 1

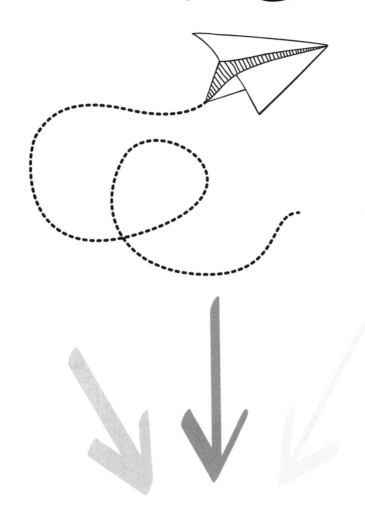

Basic Lines

Start at the dot and trace the dotted line

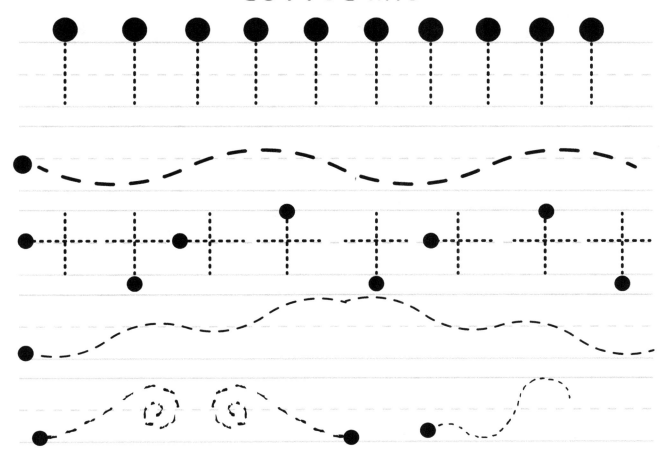

Start at the dot and catch the fly!

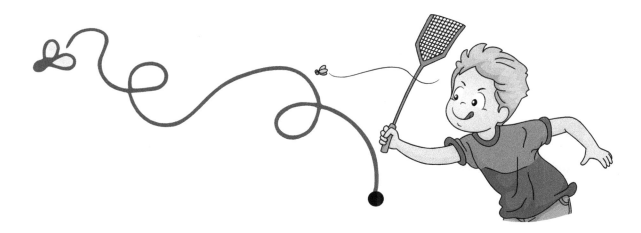

Start at the dot and trace the dotted line

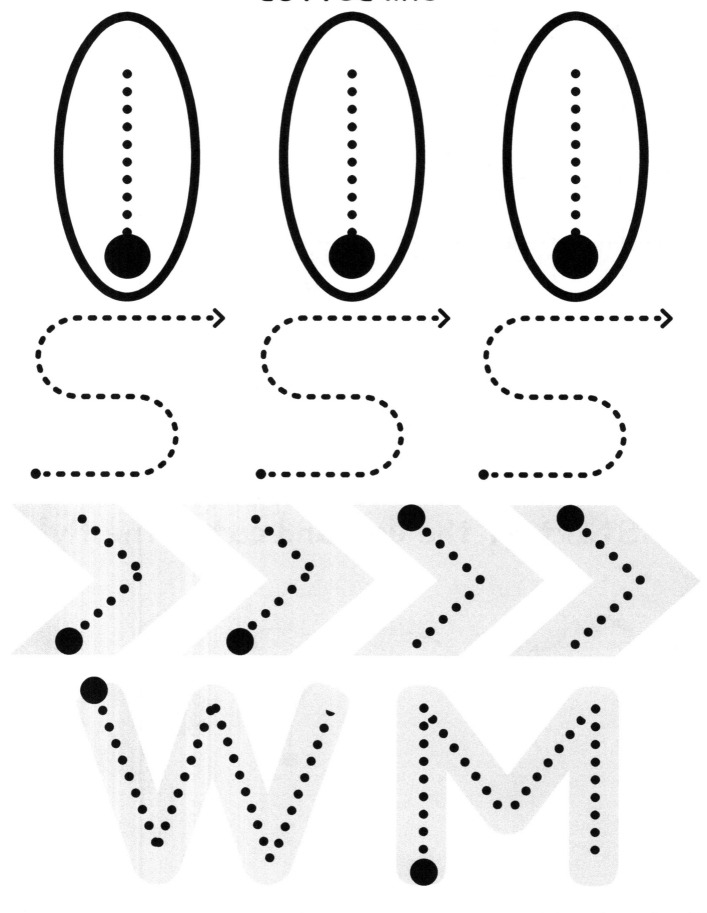

Start at the dot and follow the line to the plane

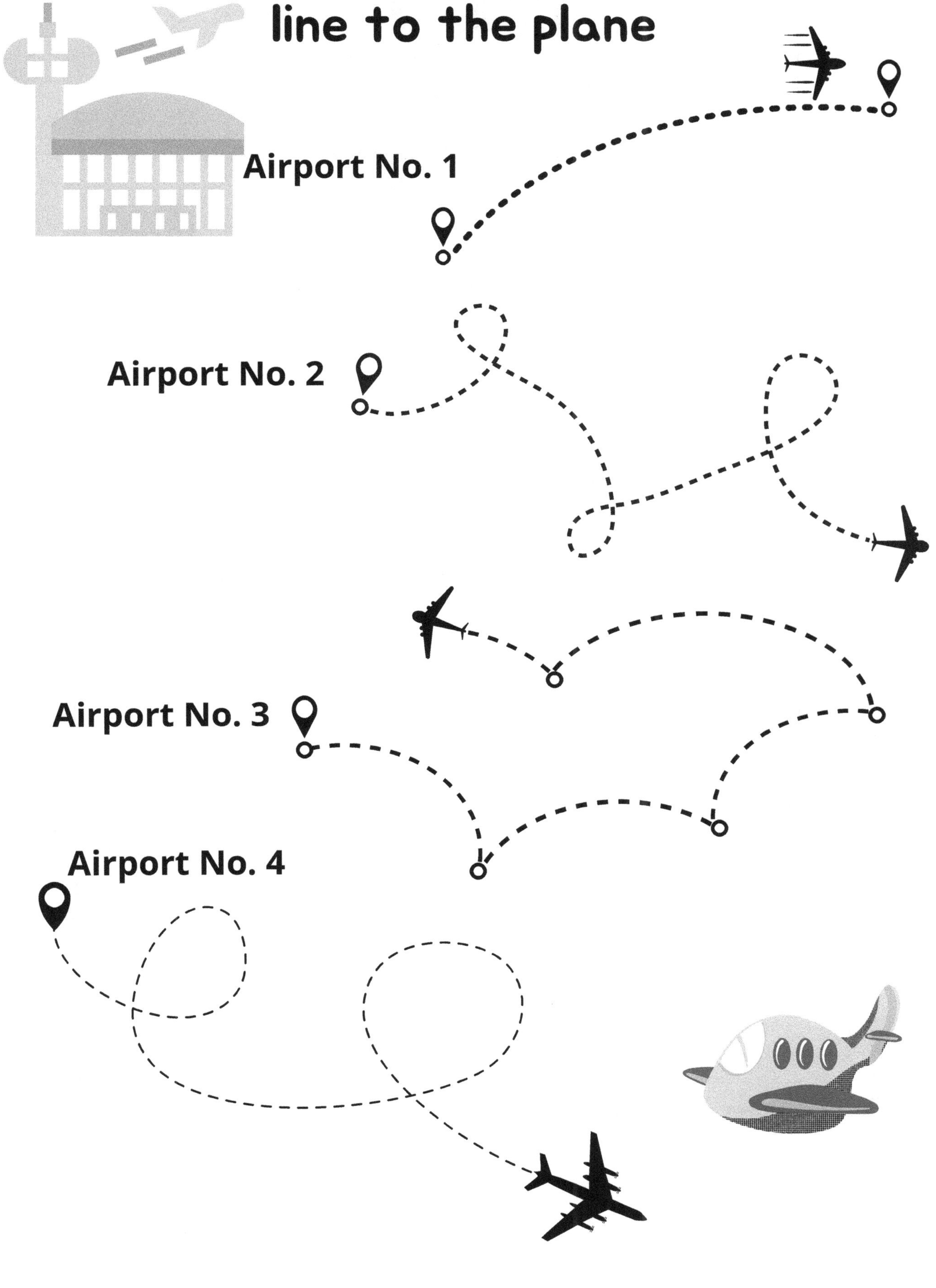

Airport No. 1

Airport No. 2

Airport No. 3

Airport No. 4

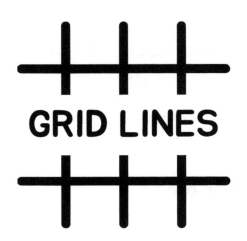

GRID LINES

GRID LINES

Can you place an X in each of the squares below?

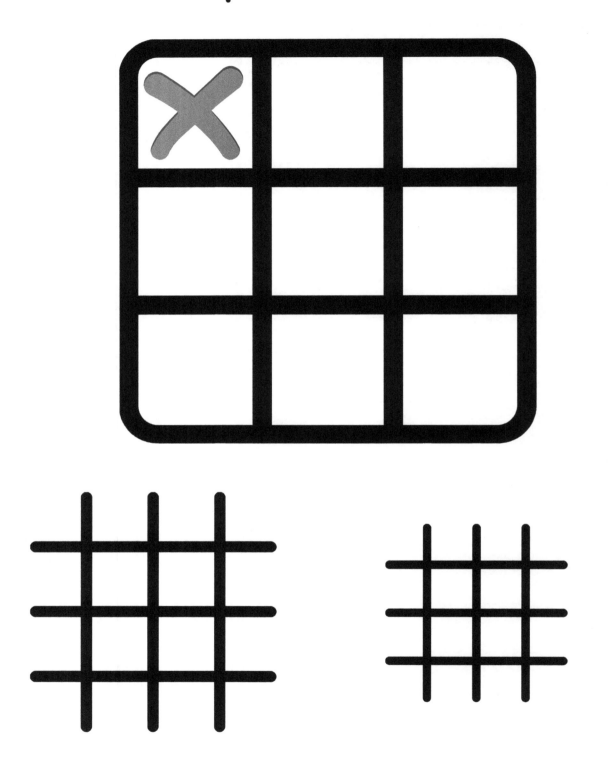

Can you trace the circles as they get smaller?

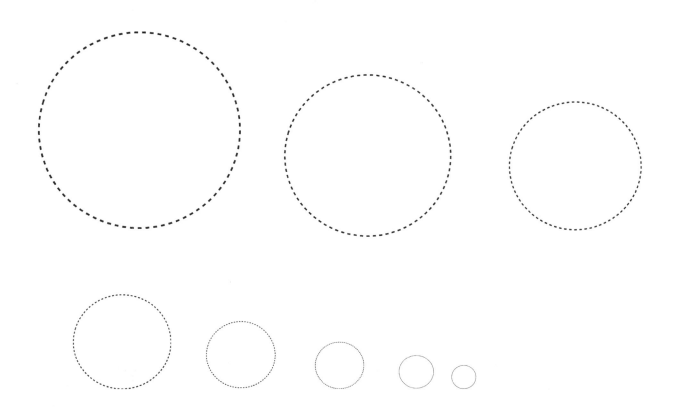

Color in the Dart Board below

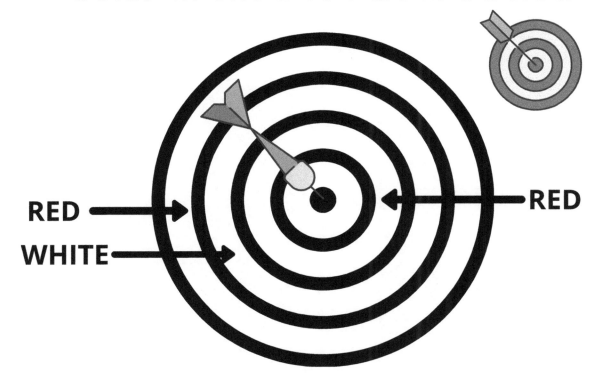

RED

RED

WHITE

SECTION 2

Basic Shapes

Start by tracing the shapes

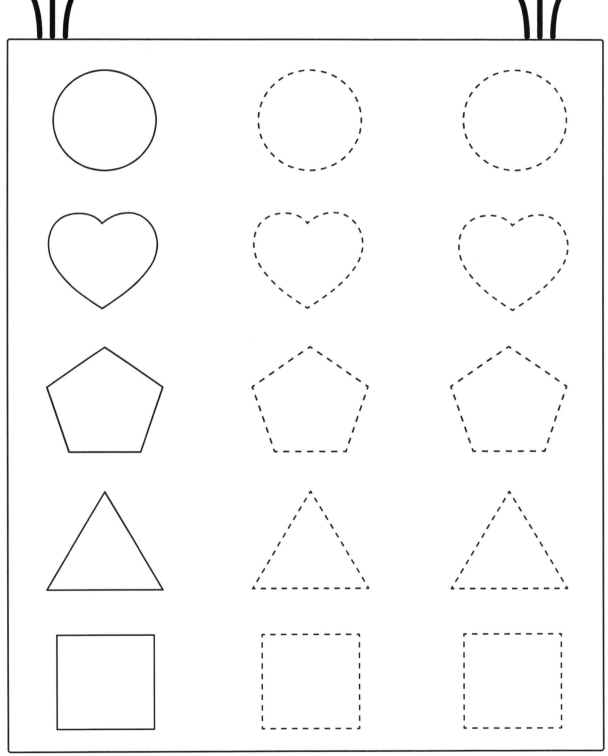

Trace the shapes

Can you draw the shape of the house?

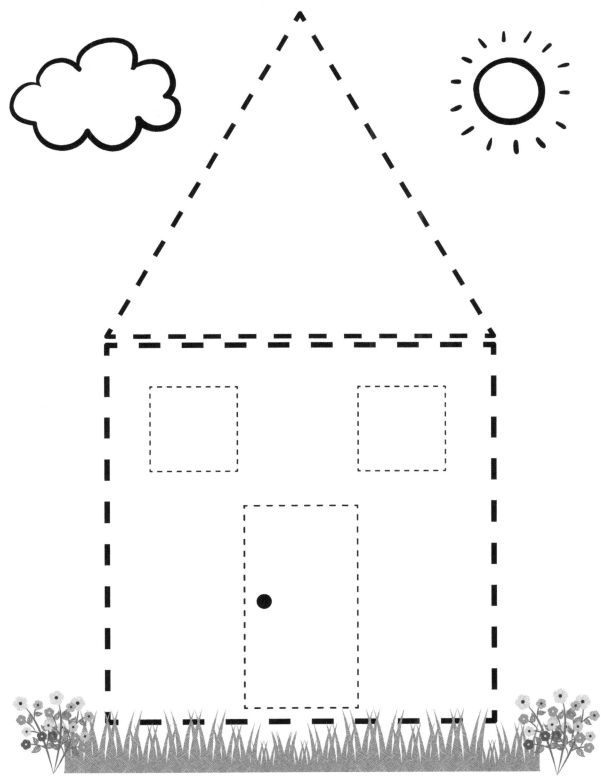

Draw a line to the treasure

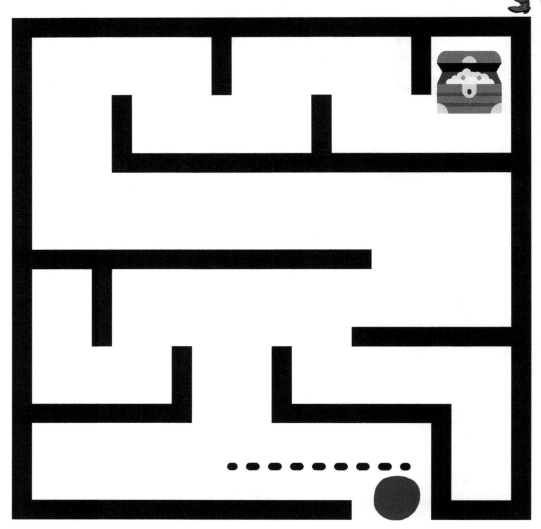

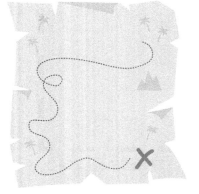

START

Race Your Car!

Start at the car and trace along the line.
Remember to keep on the road!

RACE 1

RACE 2

RACE 4

RACE 3

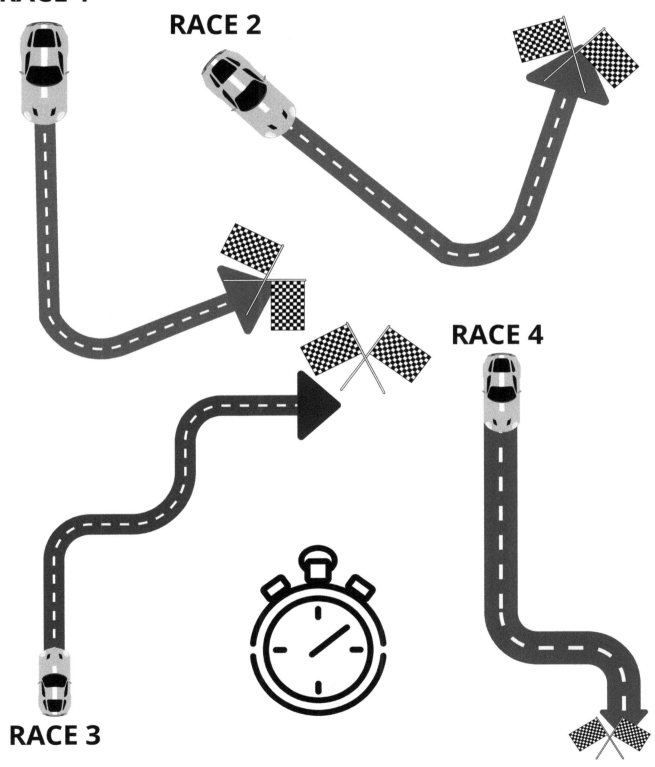

Keep inside the lines

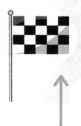

SECTION 3

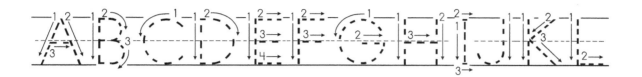

Letter Formation

Tip:

Follow the numbers
and letters on each
example like this! →

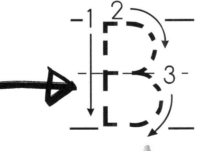

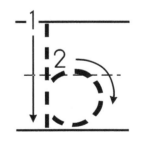

LETTER

 **A**nt

Try the letters yourself in the space below

LETTER

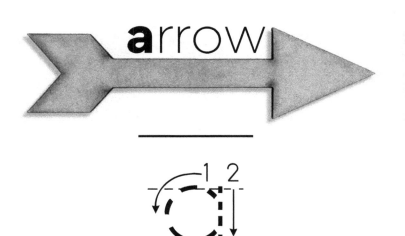

Try the letters yourself in the space below

LETTER

 **B**ee

B

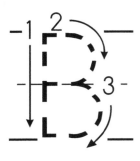

B B B B B B B B

B B B B B B B B

B B B B B B B B

B B B B B B B B

B B B B B B B B

Try the letters yourself in the space below

LETTER

bear

b b b b b b b b b

b b b b b b b b b

b b b b b b b b b

b b b b b b b b b

b b b b b b b b b

Try the letters yourself in the space below

LETTER

 **c**lock

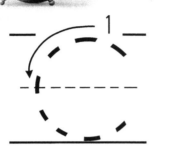

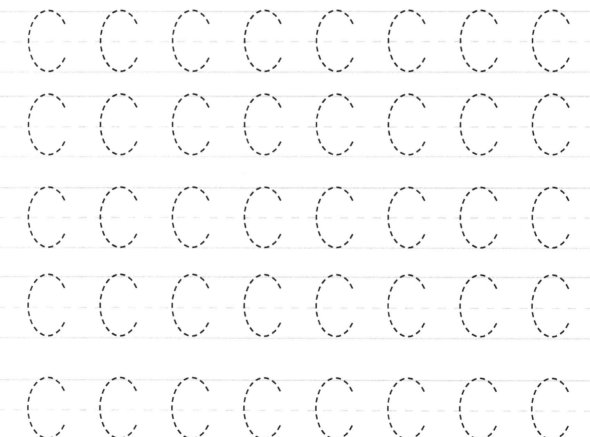

Try the letters yourself in the space below

LETTER

 **c**at

C

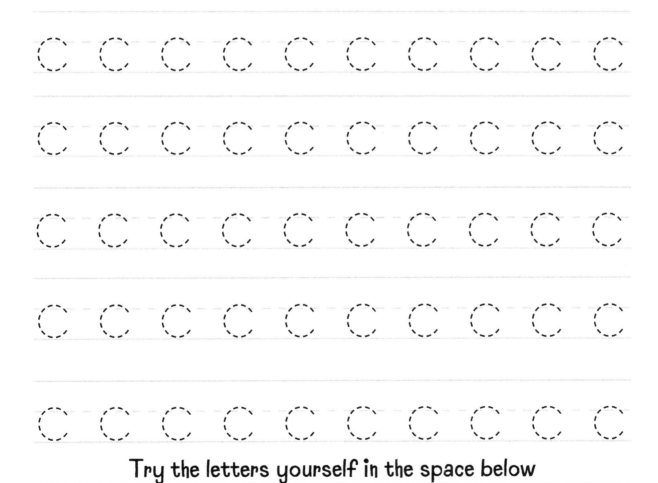

Try the letters yourself in the space below

LETTER

Dog

D D D D D D D D

D D D D D D D D

D D D D D D D D

D D D D D D D D

D D D D D D D D

Try the letters yourself in the space below

LETTER

 **d**rum

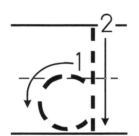

Try the letters yourself in the space below

LETTER

Elephant

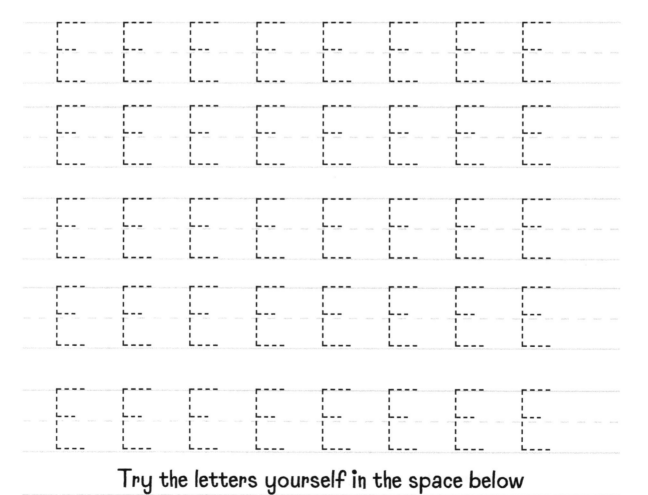

Try the letters yourself in the space below

LETTER

 **e**gg

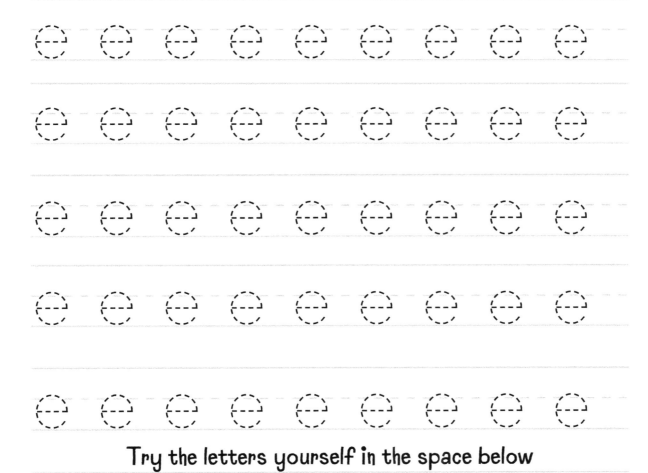

Try the letters yourself in the space below

LETTER

F|y

Try the letters yourself in the space below

LETTER

frog

Try the letters yourself in the space below

LETTER

 **G**oat

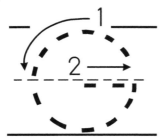

G

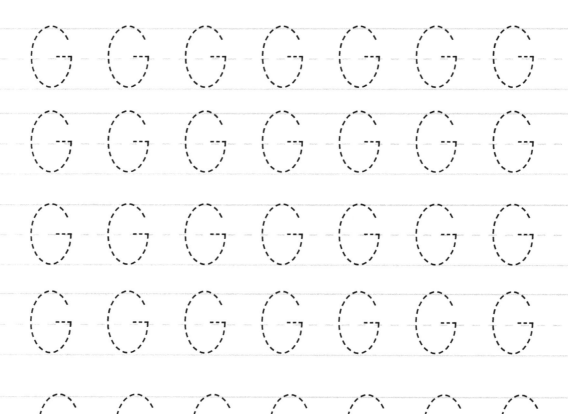

Try the letters yourself in the space below

LETTER

giraffe

g g g g g g g g g

g g g g g g g g g

g g g g g g g g g

g g g g g g g g g

g g g g g g g g g

Try the letters yourself in the space below

LETTER

 Helicopter

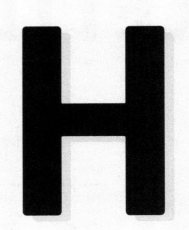

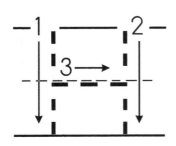

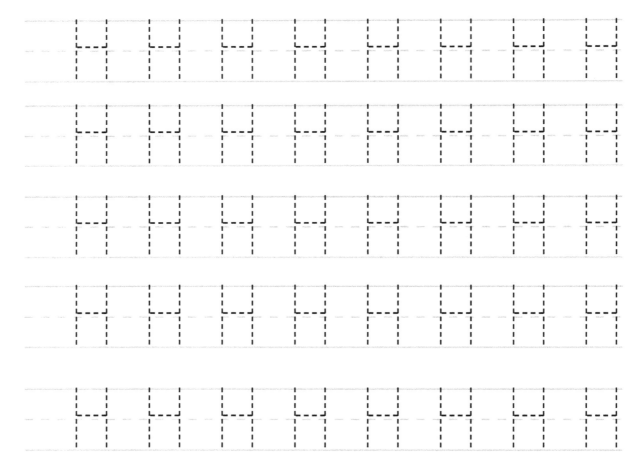

Try the letters yourself in the space below

LETTER

 **h**at

 h

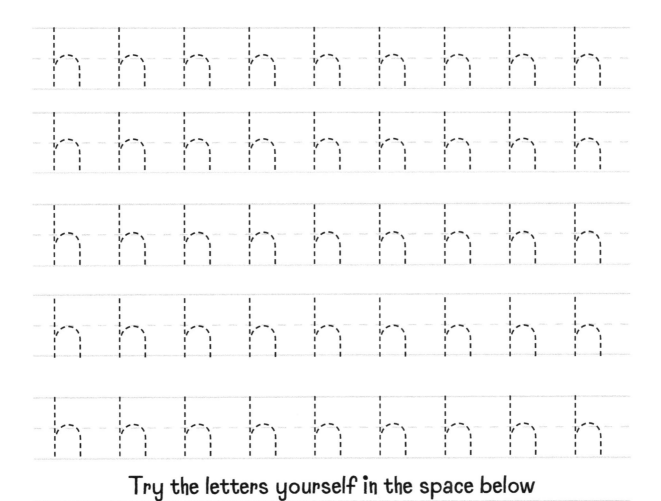

Try the letters yourself in the space below

LETTER

 **I**gloo

I

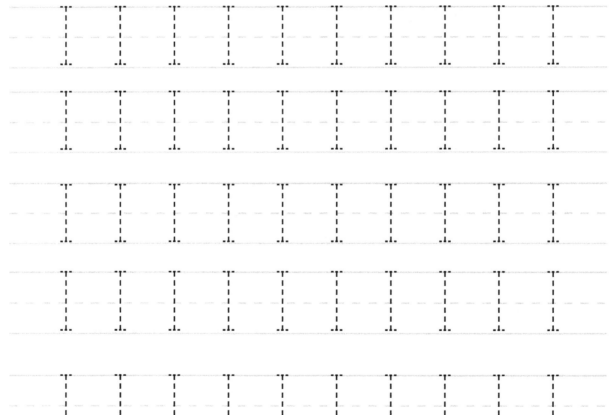

Try the letters yourself in the space below

LETTER

  **i**nsect

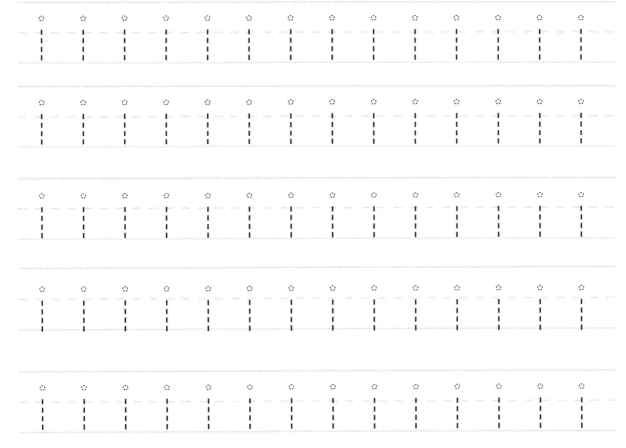

Try the letters yourself in the space below

LETTER

Jaguar

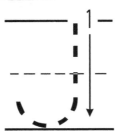

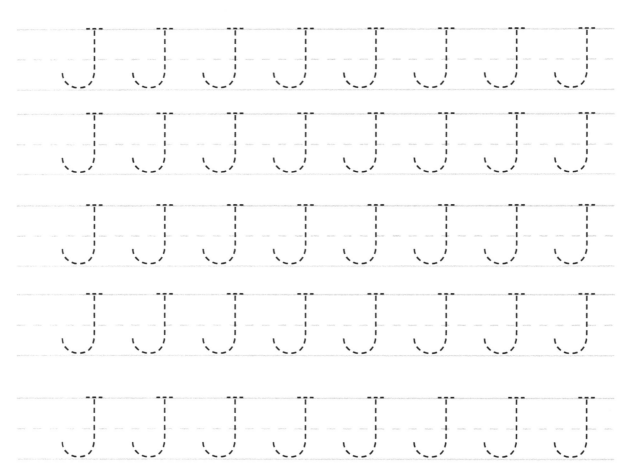

Try the letters yourself in the space below

LETTER

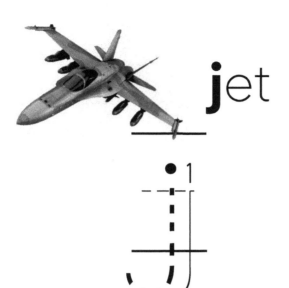

jet

j

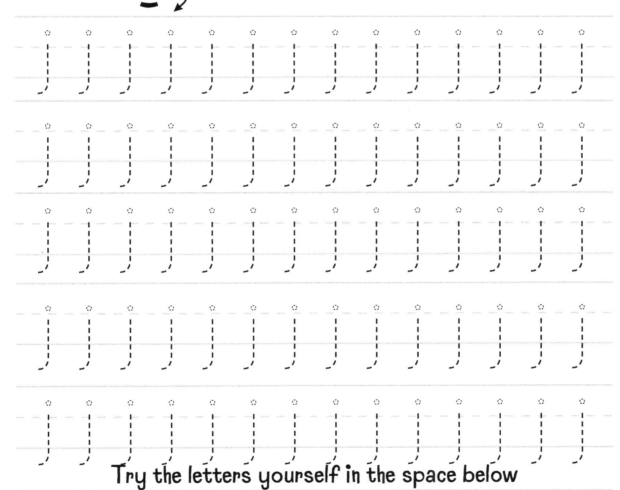

Try the letters yourself in the space below

LETTER

 **K**ite

K

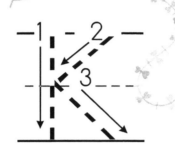

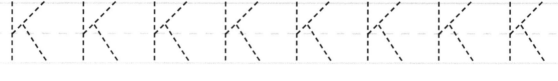

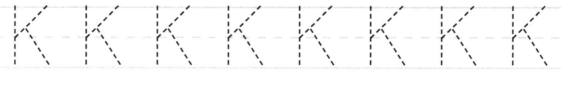

Try the letters yourself in the space below

LETTER

koala

k k k k k k k k k k

k k k k k k k k k k

k k k k k k k k k k

k k k k k k k k k k

k k k k k k k k k k

Try the letters yourself in the space below

LETTER

 **L**emon

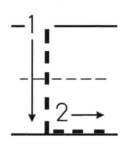

Try the letters yourself in the space below

LETTER

lizard

l

Try the letters yourself in the space below

LETTER

♪ **M**usic

M

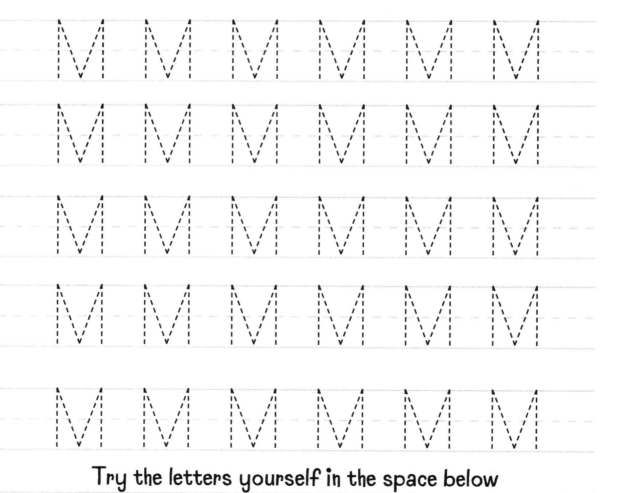

Try the letters yourself in the space below

LETTER

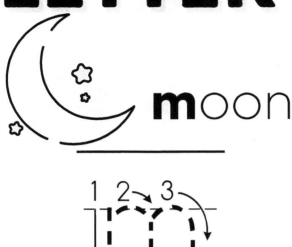

moon

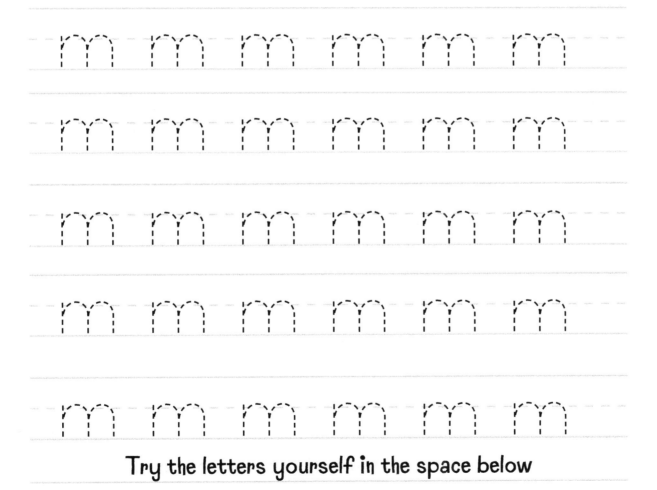

Try the letters yourself in the space below

LETTER

Nest

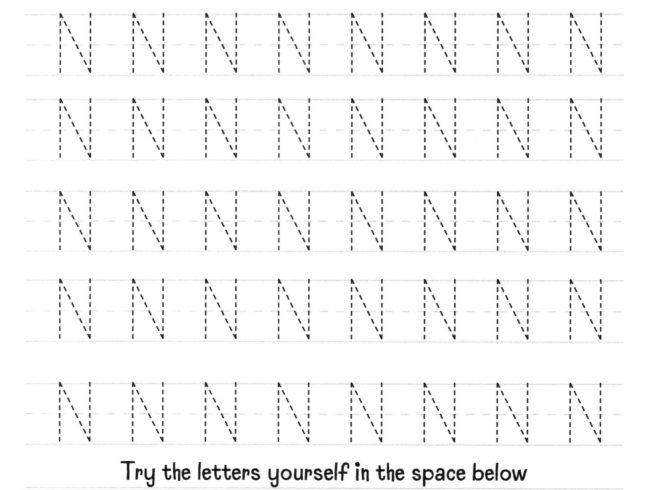

Try the letters yourself in the space below

LETTER

 **n**ail

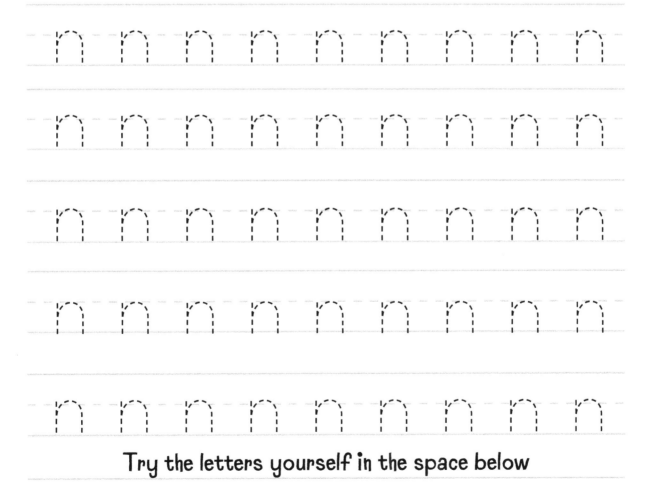

Try the letters yourself in the space below

LETTER

 **O**range

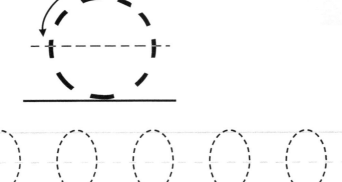

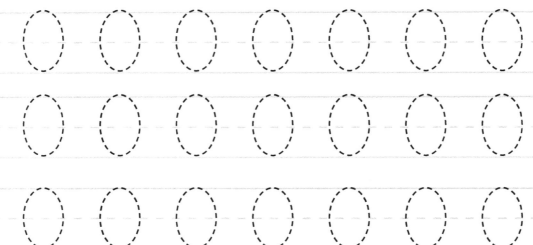

Try the letters yourself in the space below

LETTER

 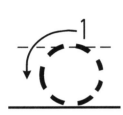 **o**ctopus

 O

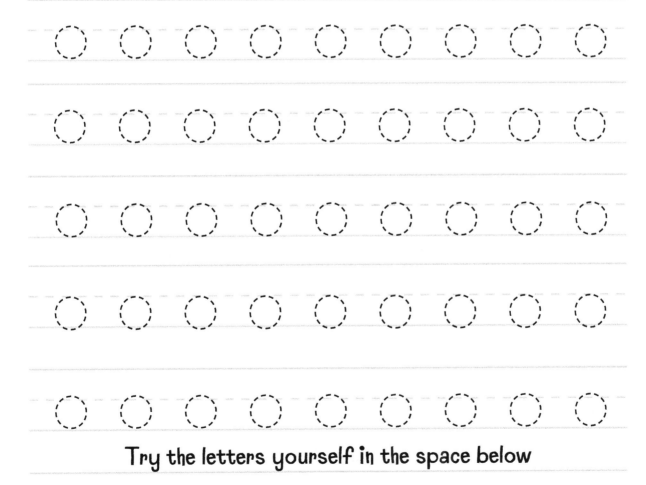

Try the letters yourself in the space below

LETTER

Pig

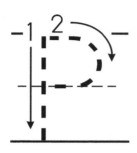

P P P P P P P P P

P P P P P P P P P

P P P P P P P P P

P P P P P P P P P

P P P P P P P P P

Try the letters yourself in the space below

LETTER

pencil

p

1 2

p p p p p p p p

p p p p p p p p

p p p p p p p p

p p p p p p p p

p p p p p p p p

Try the letters yourself in the space below

LETTER

 **Q**ueen

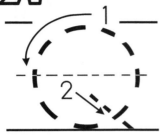

Try the letters yourself in the space below

LETTER

 **q**uiet

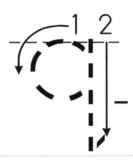

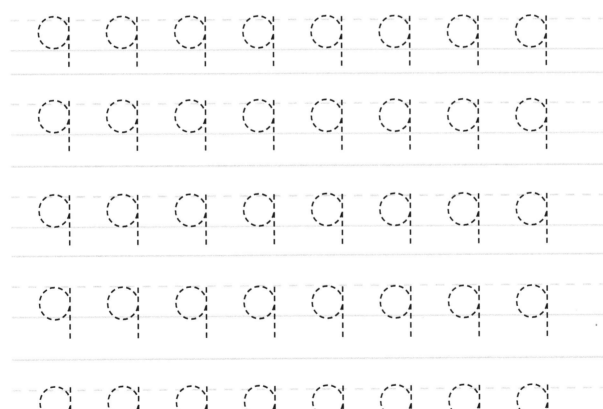

Try the letters yourself in the space below

LETTER

Rooster

R R R R R R R R

R R R R R R R R

R R R R R R R R

R R R R R R R R

R R R R R R R R

Try the letters yourself in the space below

LETTER

 **r**ope

_____

r r r r r r r r r r r r r

r r r r r r r r r r r r r

r r r r r r r r r r r r r

r r r r r r r r r r r r r

r r r r r r r r r r r r r

Try the letters yourself in the space below

LETTER

Ship

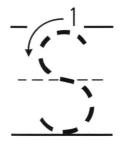

S S S S S S S S

S S S S S S S S

S S S S S S S S

S S S S S S S S

S S S S S S S S

Try the letters yourself in the space below

LETTER

scissors

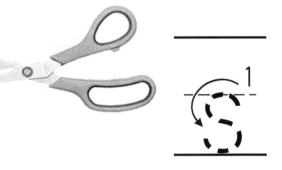

Try the letters yourself in the space below

LETTER

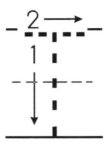

Tiger

Try the letters yourself in the space below

LETTER

turtle

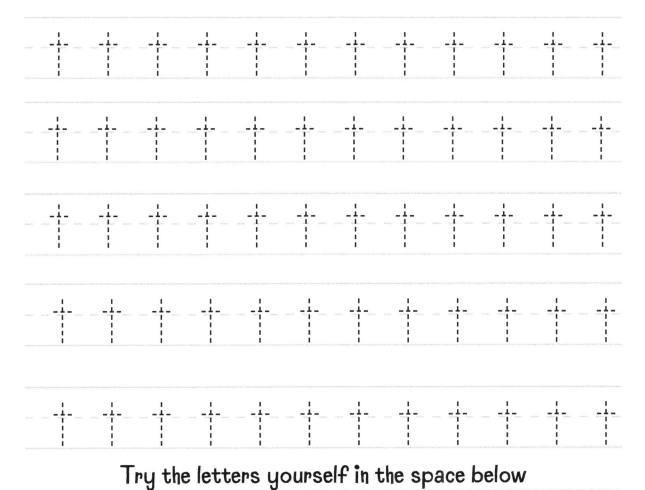

Try the letters yourself in the space below

LETTER

Umbrella

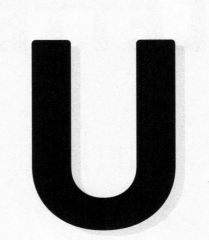

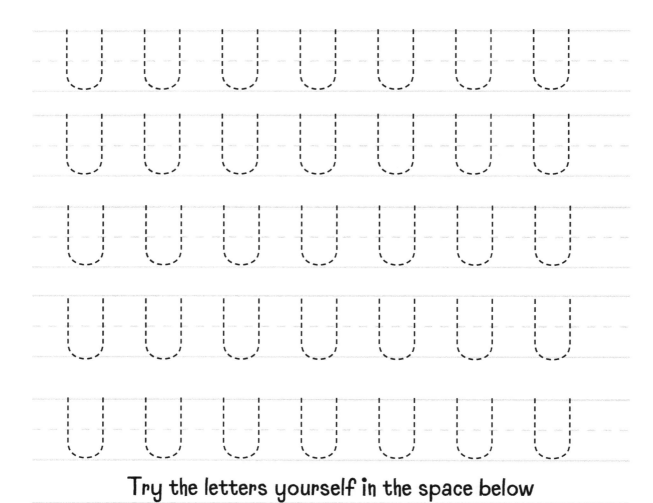

Try the letters yourself in the space below

LETTER

unicycle

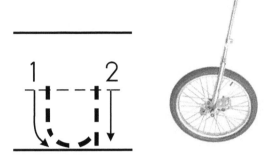

u

u u u u u u u u u

u u u u u u u u u

u u u u u u u u u

u u u u u u u u u

u u u u u u u u u u

Try the letters yourself in the space below

LETTER

Violin

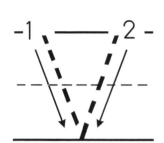
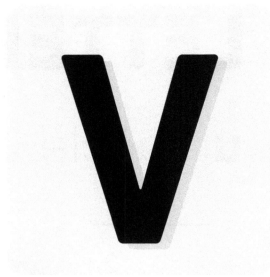

Try the letters yourself in the space below

LETTER

volcano

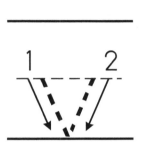

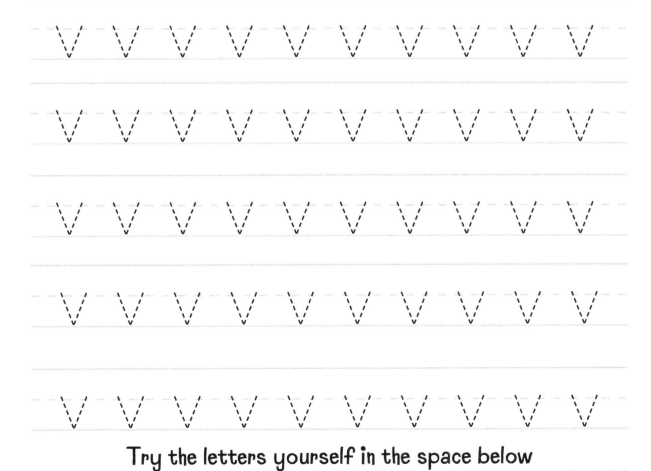

Try the letters yourself in the space below

LETTER

 **W**hale

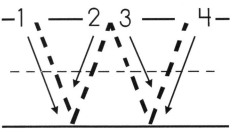

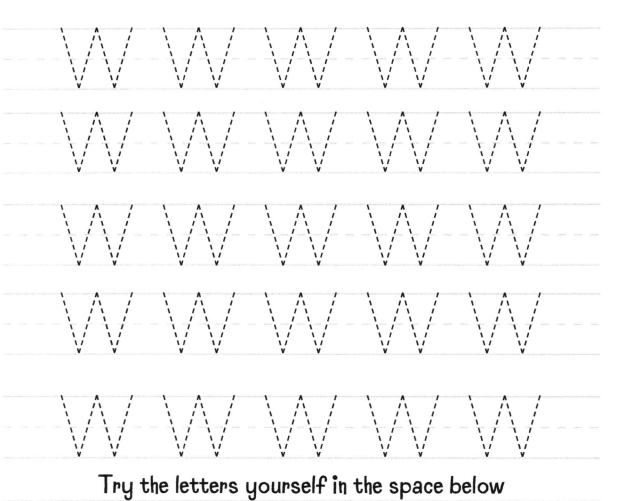

Try the letters yourself in the space below

LETTER

watermelon

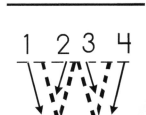

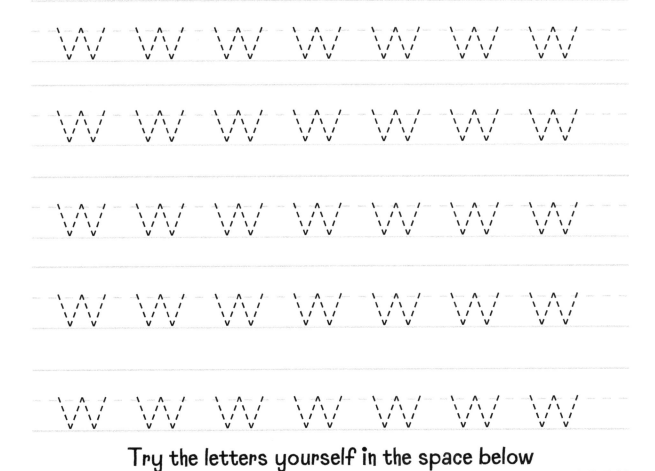

Try the letters yourself in the space below

LETTER

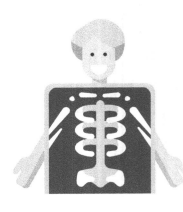

X-ray

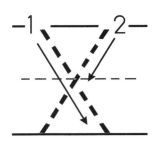

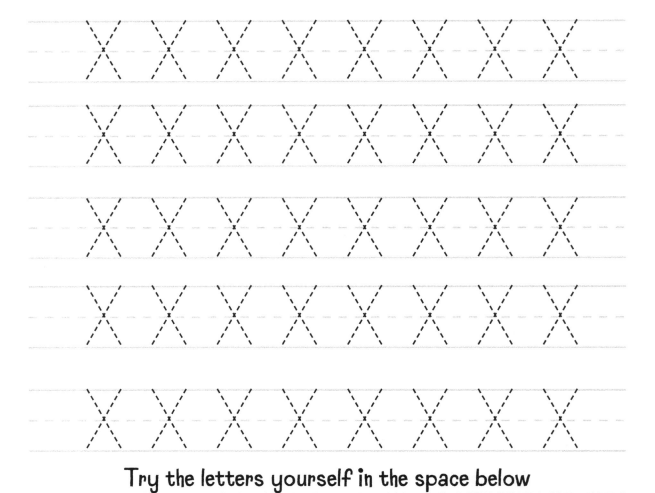

Try the letters yourself in the space below

LETTER

xylophone

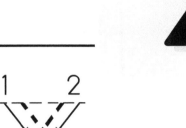

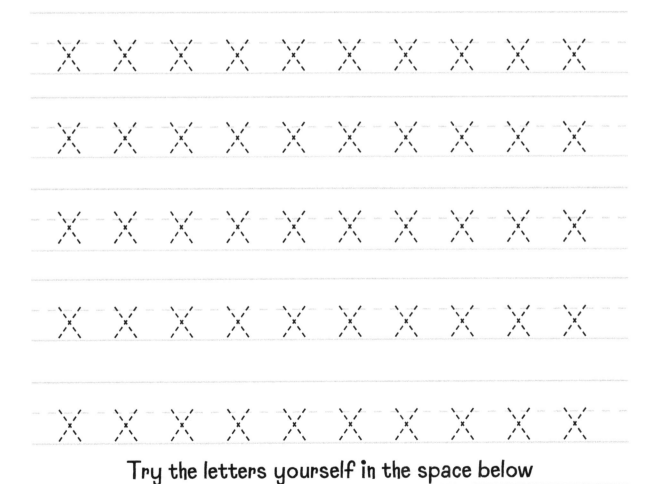

Try the letters yourself in the space below

LETTER

Yolk

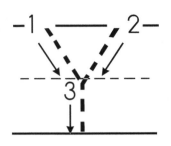

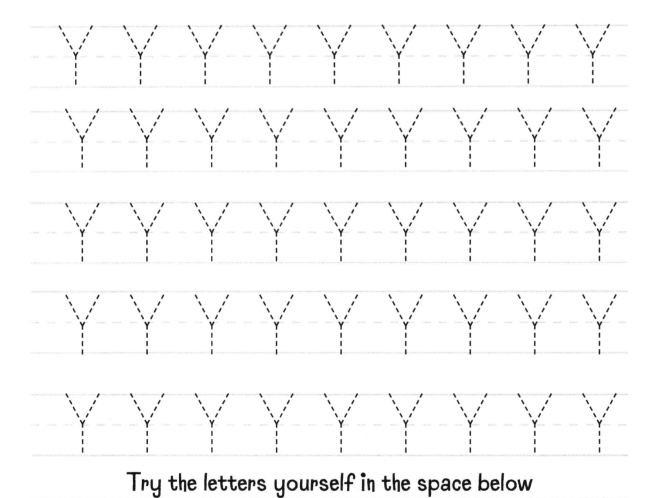

Try the letters yourself in the space below

LETTER

yawn

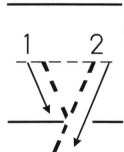

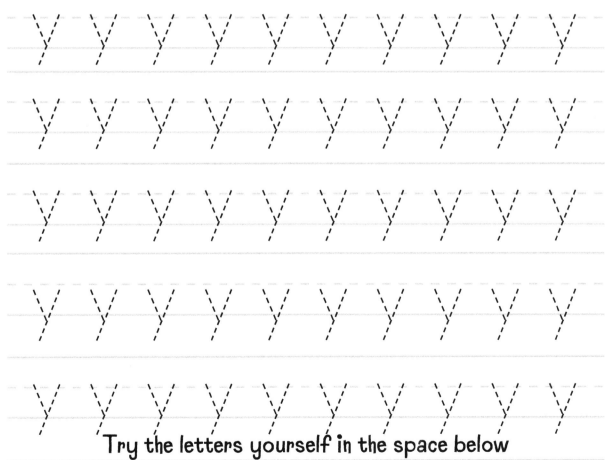

Try the letters yourself in the space below

LETTER

ZOO

Zoo

Z

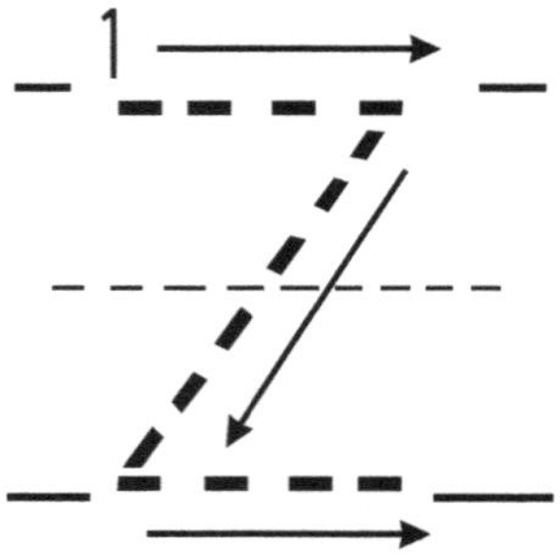

Try the letters yourself in the space below

LETTER

zebra

Z

1 →

z

z z z z z z z z z z

z z z z z z z z z z

z z z z z z z z z z

z z z z z z z z z z

z z z z z z z z z z

Try the letters yourself in the space below

EXTRA ACTIVITIES

For kids that would like some more letter and writing practice

Tracing Letters

Practice writing the alphabet by tracing the letters below.

Aa   Bb   Cc   Dd

Ee   Ff   Gg   Hh

Ii   Jj   Kk   Ll

Mm   Nn   Oo   Pp

Qq   Rr   Ss   Tt

Uu   Vv   Ww   Xx

Yy   Zz

Practice Here

Aa Aa Aa Aa Aa

Bb Bb Bb Bb Bb

Cc Cc Cc Cc Cc

Dd Dd Dd Dd Dd

Ee Ee Ee Ee Ee

Ff Ff Ff Ff Ff

Gg Gg Gg Gg Gg

Practice Here

Practice Here

Practice Here

Practice Here

The friendly cat

The barking dog

The hungry fox

I love vegetables

The zoo is fun

We walk to school

The big mountain

Trace the words

I can write

The brown fox

I love to play

I love story time

Rabbits run fast

Today is sunny

Tomorrow is raining

The sky is blue

I can write neatly

Days of the week

Trace the letters to spell out the days.

Sunday

Monday

Tuesday

Wednesday

Thursday

Friday

Saturday

Trace the words

Test out your writing here!

One

Two

Three

Four

Five

Six

Seven

Eight

Nine and Ten

Things we see in school

Trace the words and then see if you can write them in the space next to it.

Books

Bag

Pencil

Crayons

Glue

Eraser

Practice Writing

Test out your writing here!

CERTIFICATE OF COMPLETION

FOR LEARNING TO WRITE

Congratulations

NAME: _____

AGE: _____

DATE: _____

Signature _____

You may also be interested in:

Available on all major online bookstores

The Life
Graduate

PUBLISHING GROUP

Thank you for your purchase of this book. It is greatly appreciated.

I founded The Life Graduate Publishing Group in early 2019 with the key focus being the creation of high-quality books and resources that will benefit customers worldwide.

The company has now expanded with over 200 titles ranging from self-help books, children's books, journals, diaries, educational resources and sporting resources. The Life Graduate Publishing Group is tailoring resources specific to the needs of the customer with an ever growing bookstore.

The Life Graduate Publishing Group uses the world's largest Print on Demand (POD) services and therefore our books are available to anybody, anywhere in the world.

Should you like to purchase further books that are available through The Life Graduate Publishing Group, then please visit us at via the following:

Website: www.thelifegraduate.com
Facebook: @thelifegraduategroup · Publisher
Instagram: thelifegraduate

All the best,

Romney Nelson

Founder - The Life Graduate Publishing Group

Ingram Content Group UK Ltd.
Milton Keynes UK
UKHW031823090323
418309UK00012B/693